Carol Lines to Hymn

By John L. Hoh, Jr.

Copyright © 2007, 2008, John L. Hoh, Jr. All rights reserved
ISBN 978-0-6151-8543-9

HoneyMilk Publications
7253 N. 86th. St., Suite 201
Milwaukee WI 53224

HoneyMilk

Publications

Fine publications of a spiritual nature

Introduction

Christmas is a special time. One of the aspects of
Christmas that seems to make it special are the hymns and
carols of the season.

Most singers of every persuasion issues a Christmas
album. I have a tendency to acquire Christmas CDs to the
point that many only get played once a year, or maybe
every other year. Of course I have favorites that are played
almost daily after Thanksgiving until about January 6 or 7.
January 6 is celebrated in the Western (Latin) Churches as
Epiphany; January 7 is celebrated as Christmas among the
Eastern Rite (Greek) Churches.

This book features several Christmas carols I have come to
know and love. I have written meditations on these carols
to reflect even deeper on the miracle of the season, that
God would take on human flesh and actually live among us
and with us and be born in lowly circumstances to poor
people. Imagine, the Lord and King of the Universe born a

helpless baby and reliant on the protection of human parents! (Granted, these parents had divine help what with angelic warnings and dreams. But even here there was a trust that the parents would do the right thing.)

The book is divided into three parts.

The first part looks at the four Biblical Christmas Songs. These songs are the Song of Mary, the Song of Zechariah, the Song of the Angels, and the Song of Simeon.

The second part features carols from antiquity and the Reformation and Renaissance era.

The third part features more contemporary Praises pertinent to the Christmas season.

It is my hope and prayer that you, dear reader, enjoy the beauty, majesty, and message of these carols that sing praises to the baby in Bethlehem, our Lord and King and Savior.

Contents

Christmas Carol Questions

Biblical Songs
Song of Mary
Song of Zechariah
Song of the Angels
Song of Simeon

Ancient Hymns
Of The Father's Love Begotten
Songs of Thankfulness and Praise
From Heaven Above to Earth I Come
Jesu, Joy of Man's Desiring
Hark the Herald Angels Sing
Hark! Felix Mendelssohn Compose

Modern Praises
>   Now the Silence/Then the Glory
>   Where Shepherds Lately Knelt
>   Someone Special
>   Before the Marvel of This Night
>   The King the Wise Men Found
>   Go, My Children, With my Blessing

Christmas Carol Answers

Christmas Carol Questions

Decipher the following clues to determine the Christmas carol being described.

1.   The initial example of a highly celebrated nativity.

2.   A felicitous emotion, directed at the entirety of the terrestrial sphere.

3.   Pass hitherward, everyone who exhibits consistency of character.

4.   A young lad whose musical talents are expressed rhythmically.

5.   The hour of its transparent occurrence coincided with the instant often associated with maximal darkness, either figurative or literal.

6. Strike with the fist, with sufficient force as to cause unconsciousness, Mr. and Mrs. Hall.

7. A nocturnal period unbroken by auditory interruptions.

8. My advice to you is to listen intently to, and heed, the heavenly messengers as they vocalize musical selections announcing an important event.

9. A significant distance from here, within the confines of a feeding trough for animals.

10. The auditory sensation of roughly spherical sound-making objects, vibrating in a resonant fashion, followed by the name of the objects themselves.

11. Our sincere desire for you is for your yuletide celebration to be an enjoyable one.

12. A dozen terrestrial rotational time periods, signifying a series of steps leading up to, and ushering in, the celebration of the Nativity.

13. The benevolent senior nobility whose name I shan't say because it would give away the answer to this puzzle.

14. A verbal utterance, addressed toward a coniferous member of the plant family, often used as the centerpiece of yuletide gatherings.

15. Multiple highly polished, colorless, metallic, cup-shaped devices that give forth a ringing sound when struck.

16. Celestial heralds at a great altitude; specifically, those whose announcements have already been listened to and understood by us.

17. Haste hence, and publish the news in the Alpine, Nordic, Appalachian, Rocky, and/or Himalayan regions.

18. May the Almighty grant to you a recuperative repose, all you festive males of chivalrous character.

19. The original utterance, as well as a repetition, of a plea for the arrival of the One whose presence brings God Himself to us.

20. There exists in the atmosphere a musical selection.

21. During the dimly-lit extent of time wherein those persons who enjoyed a bucolic relationship with the domesticated stock in their charge, monitored them for their safekeeping.

22. Enlighten me as to the identity of this offspring.

23. The trio of us, the most authoritative examples of monarchical governmental leadership.

24. A temporal duration characterized by reverence, awe, and the sun's position being beneath the horizon.

25. From a celestial locale, one over our heads, to a terrestrial locale I arrive.

Carol Lines to Hymn

Biblical Songs

Carol Lines to Hymn

Song of Mary
(Magnificat)

Luke 1:46-55
(New International Version [NIV])
And Mary said: "My soul glorifies the Lord and my spirit rejoices in God my Savior, for he has been mindful of the humble state of his servant. From now on all generations will call me blessed, for the Mighty One has done great things for me- holy is his name. His mercy extends to those who fear him, from generation to generation. He has performed mighty deeds with his arm; he has scattered those who are proud in their inmost thoughts. He has brought down rulers from their thrones

Luke 1:46-55
(New International Version [NIV])
but has lifted up the humble. He has filled the hungry with good things but has sent the rich away empty. He has helped his servant Israel, remembering to be merciful to Abraham and his descendants forever, even as he said to our fathers."

This section begins with the first in the series of Biblical Christmas songs, the Song of Mary. It is also known as the *Magnificat*, which is the first word of the song in Latin. "Magnificat" means "[it] glorifies" as the Latin, roughly translated, is "my heart glorifies."

At this point, stop and consider Mary's plight. She is probably a teenager. She is a devout Jewish girl who doesn't "play with the boys." She is visited by a stranger and is told by this bright, frightful stranger that she will have a baby, a baby from *Jahweh* himself! How would you respond?

At one time in our societal history "wayward" girls often went out of town to visit an "aunt." This was a euphemism that an unmarried woman was with child and she was away from society's eyes and gossiping tongues, which would surely wag. When the child was born and placed for adoption, the young lady returned home with dignity, if not conscience, intact.

So where could Mary go? Her marriage to Joseph hadn't been formally tied in a marriage ceremony. Very likely Joseph was still working on their home—a home that had to be approved by his father before the marriage could take place! Add to that the Mosaic Law's decree that one caught in adultery should be stoned. Now, granted, Roman occupation meant the Jews had no control over capital punishment, but who would raise questions if a young, "sullied" lady from a small town in backwoods Galilee went missing?

But the angel gives Mary a clue that the message he bears is true and valid. He directs Mary to her cousin, the aged Elizabeth who is well past the age of child-bearing. The angel states that this Elizabeth is also pregnant (for six months, actually). Thus Mary has someone she can turn to and stay with. And at six months, the physical evidence of the older woman's pregnancy would be visible.

So Mary goes not to be with an "aunt" but to be with her cousin. Neither lady expected these turns of events. But here they were, vessels of God's love. One is carrying the forerunner to the Messiah; the other carries the Messiah himself.

And when Mary arrives at the Zechariah residence, her doubts are silenced and the angel's message confirmed. Her cousin, Elizabeth, is with child. Not only that, but the child within Elizabeth is moved by the Spirit to leap with joy in the presence of His Savior.

And so Mary knows she need not fear. The God whom she carries in her womb will protect her from any harm. The birth pains she will experience will all too soon be replaced by the piercing of her heart as she would watch her son die on the cross.

She will be called blessed, not because she was special or sinless but because God had grace on her. Mary says: "My soul glorifies the Lord and my spirit rejoices in God my

Savior, for he has been mindful of the humble state of his servant." Mary speaks of a savior, a savior she wouldn't need if she were sinless. She also speaks of her "humble state" and speaks of being a "servant." The Greek word used here is *doula* (δουλα), the feminine form of *doulos* (δουλος), which Paul used when referring to himself as "servant of Christ Jesus." The term *doulos* stands in stark contrast to another Greek word for slave, *paidos* (παιδος). A *paidos* was a lowly slave, one who couldn't be trusted. A *doulos* (*doula*) was a slave or servant who had earned the trust of the master, who often kept the books, educated the children, and ran the households. Mary is acknowledging that she was entrusted with carrying out a part of God's grace.

Mary also displays a knowledge of the Old Testament Scriptures. The following tables illustrate the correlations in Mary's Song to Old Testament prophecies as well as to Hannah's Prayer. No doubt she listened attentively as her dad taught the Scriptures in the home.

Mary's Song	Old Testament Reference
46My soul glorifies the Lord	
47and my spirit rejoices in God my Savior,	
48for he has been mindful of the humble state of his servant. From now on all generations will call me blessed,	And she made a vow, saying, "O LORD Almighty, if you will only look upon your servant's misery and remember me, and not forget your servant but give her a son, then I will give him to the LORD for all the days of his life, and no razor will ever be used on his head." *1 Samuel 1:11*

Mary's Song	Old Testament Reference
[49]for the Mighty One has done great things for me-holy is his name.	He provided redemption for his people; he ordained his covenant forever- holy and awesome is his name. *Psalm 111:9*
[50]His mercy extends to those who fear him, from generation to generation.	As a father has compassion on his children, so the LORD has compassion on those who fear him...But from everlasting to everlasting the LORD's love is with those who fear him, and his righteousness with their children's children *Psalm 103:13, 17*
[51]He has performed mighty deeds with his arm; he has scattered those who are proud in their inmost thoughts.	You crushed Rahab like one of the slain; with your strong arm you scattered your enemies. *Psalm 89:10* You save the humble, but your eyes are on the haughty to bring them low. *2 Samuel 22:28*
[52]He has brought down rulers from their thrones but has lifted up the humble.	He leads priests away stripped and overthrows men long established. *Job 12:19* The lowly he sets on high, and those who mourn are lifted to safety. *Job 5:11*
[53]He has filled the hungry with good things but has sent the rich away empty.	Those who were full hire themselves out for food, but those who were hungry hunger no more. She who was barren has borne seven children, but she who has had many sons pines away. *1 Samuel 2:5* for he satisfies the thirsty and fills the hungry with good things. *Psalm 107:9*

Mary's Song	Old Testament Reference
[54]He has helped his servant Israel, remembering to be merciful	He has remembered his love and his faithfulness to the house of Israel; all the ends of the earth have seen the salvation of our God. *Psalm 98:3* "But you, O Israel, my servant, Jacob, whom I have chosen, you descendants of Abraham my friend, I took you from the ends of the earth, from its farthest corners I called you. I said, 'You are my servant'; I have chosen you and have not rejected you. *Isaiah 41:8, 9*
[55]to Abraham and his descendants forever, even as he said to our fathers.	You will be true to Jacob, and show mercy to Abraham, as you pledged on oath to our fathers in days long ago. *Micah 7:20* I will establish my covenant as an everlasting covenant between me and you and your descendants after you for the generations to come, to be your God and the God of your descendants after you. *Genesis 17:7* I will surely bless you and make your descendants as numerous as the stars in the sky and as the sand on the seashore. Your descendants will take possession of the cities of their enemies, and through your offspring all nations on earth will be blessed, because you have obeyed me." *Genesis 22:17, 18*

Mary's Song	Hannah's Prayer
My soul glorifies the Lord and my spirit rejoices in God my Savior, for he has been mindful of the humble state of his servant. From now on all generations will call me blessed, for the Mighty One has done great things for me-holy is his name. His mercy extends to those who fear him, from generation to generation. He has performed mighty deeds with his arm; he has scattered those who are proud in their inmost thoughts. He has brought down rulers from their thrones but has lifted up the humble. He has filled the hungry with good things but has sent the rich away empty. He has helped his servant Israel, remembering to be merciful to Abraham and his descendants forever, even as he said to our fathers.	Then Hannah prayed and said: "My heart rejoices in the LORD; in the LORD my horn is lifted high. My mouth boasts over my enemies, for I delight in your deliverance. There is no one holy like the LORD; there is no one besides you; there is no Rock like our God. Do not keep talking so proudly or let your mouth speak such arrogance, for the LORD is a God who knows, and by him deeds are weighed. The bows of the warriors are broken, but those who stumbled are armed with strength. Those who were full hire themselves out for food, but those who were hungry hunger no more. She who was barren has borne seven children, but she who has had many sons pines away. The LORD brings death and makes alive; he brings down to the grave and raises up. The LORD sends poverty and wealth; he humbles and he exalts. He raises the poor from the dust and lifts the needy from the ash heap; he seats them with princes and has them inherit a throne of honor. For the foundations of the earth are the LORD's; upon them he has set the world. He will guard the feet of his saints, but the wicked will be silenced in darkness. It is not by strength that one prevails; those who oppose the LORD will be shattered. He will thunder against them from heaven; the LORD will judge the ends of the earth. He will give strength to his king and exalt the horn of his anointed." *1 Samuel 2:1-10*

Carol Lines to Hymn

Song of Zechariah (Benedictus)

Luke 1:67-79
(New International Version [NIV])
His [John the Baptizer's] father Zechariah was filled with the Holy Spirit and prophesied: "Praise be to the Lord, the God of Israel, because he has come and has redeemed his people. He has raised up a horn of salvation for us in the house of his servant David (as he said through his holy prophets of long ago), salvation from our enemies and from the hand of all who hate us- to show mercy to our fathers and to remember his holy covenant, the oath he swore to our father Abraham: to rescue us from the hand of our enemies, and to enable us to serve him without fear in holiness and righteousness before him all our days. And you, my child, will be called a prophet of the Most High; for you will go on before the Lord to prepare the way

Luke 1:67-79
(New International Version [NIV])
for him, to give his people the knowledge of salvation through the forgiveness of their sins, because of the tender mercy of our God, by which the rising sun will come to us from heaven to shine on those living in darkness and in the shadow of death, to guide our feet into the path of peace."

Mary's Song came when her pregnancy with God's Son was confirmed. Zechariah's Song comes after the birth and dedication of his son. Of course Zechariah was at a disadvantage. He was struck dumb by the angel when he questioned how his aged wife could bear a child.

Zechariah, it can be argued, should know better. He was a priest and as a priest he should have known the miraculous beginnings of his race. For Abraham and his wife Sarah were also advanced in years and Isaac was born when Sarah was 90 years old! With God nothing is impossible.

And Zechariah knows his Scriptures! We will see that in a table at the end of this meditation. Several psalms come to mind in Zechariah's words: "shadow of death" and "guide our feet into the path of peace" are two examples.

Zechariah is given his voice back only when he writes the child's name: "His name is John." This simple act signifies that Zechariah acknowledges the truth of the angel's words, that this child would prepare Israel for the coming Messiah. Thus voice is given to the faith and Zechariah utters his song. The song praises God and echoes the promises made to Abraham and through the prophets.

It is interesting that the term "Israel" is used. The region where the Jews lived was known as Palestine, from the Philistines. It was Rome's way of placing a burr under the saddle of the restless Jewish people. They named the geographic area after their long-time bitter enemies. (That name remains to this day.) The provinces were called "Judea," "Samaria," and "Galilee." Some could take this as a nationalistic hope for an independent state. Or it has a spiritual significance. "Israel" is a name given to Jacob and means "one who wrestles with God." As Christians we are part of the "Israel," those who wrestle with God. Compare the list's of Israel's sons, the tribes of Israel, and the list of Israel's "tribes" in Revelation. You find three different lists: one for the sons (physical descendants of Jacob), one for the tribes (the nation of Israel), and one for the collection of saints.

The following table shows the Old Testament prophecies cited by Zechariah.

Zechariah's Song	Old Testament References
68Praise be to the Lord, the God of Israel, because he has come and has redeemed his people.	Praise be to the LORD, the God of Israel, from everlasting to everlasting. Amen and Amen. *Psalm 41:13* Praise be to the LORD God, the God of Israel, who alone does marvelous deeds. *Psalm 72:18* Praise be to the LORD, the God of Israel, from everlasting to everlasting. Let all the people say, "Amen!" Praise the LORD. *Psalm 106:48* He provided redemption for his people; he ordained his covenant forever—holy and awesome is his name. *Psalm 111:9*
69He has raised up a horn of salvation for us in the house of his servant David	The LORD is my rock, my fortress and my deliverer; my God is my rock, in whom I take refuge. He is my shield and the horn of my salvation, my stronghold. *Psalm 18:2*
70(as he said through his holy prophets of long ago),	
71salvation from our enemies and from the hand of all who hate us-	He saved them from the hand of the foe; from the hand of the enemy he redeemed them. *Psalm 106:10*

Zechariah's Song	Old Testament References
⁷²to show mercy to our fathers and to remember his holy covenant,	for their sake he remembered his covenant and out of his great love he relented. He caused them to be pitied by all who held them captive. *Psalm 106:45-46* He remembers his covenant forever, the word he commanded, for a thousand generations, the covenant he made with Abraham, the oath he swore to Isaac. *Psalm 105:8-9*
⁷³the oath he swore to our father Abraham:	I will establish my covenant as an everlasting covenant between me and you and your descendants after you for the generations to come, to be your God and the God of your descendants after you. *Genesis 17:7* I will remember my covenant with Jacob and my covenant with Isaac and my covenant with Abraham, and I will remember the land. *Leviticus 26:42*
⁷⁴to rescue us from the hand of our enemies, and to enable us to serve him without fear ...	and said, "I swear by myself, declares the LORD, that because you have done this and have not withheld your son, your only son, I will surely bless you and make your descendants as numerous as the stars in the sky and as the sand on the seashore. Your descendants will take possession of the cities of their enemies... *Genesis 22:16-17*

Zechariah's Song	Old Testament References
⁷⁵in holiness and righteousness before him all our days.	
⁷⁶And you, my child, will be called a prophet of the Most High; for you will go on before the Lord to prepare the way for him,	A voice of one calling: "In the desert prepare the way for the LORD; make straight in the wilderness a highway for our God. *Isaiah 40:3* "See, I will send my messenger, who will prepare the way before me. Then suddenly the Lord you are seeking will come to his temple; the messenger of the covenant, whom you desire, will come," says the LORD Almighty. *Malachi 3:1*
⁷⁷to give his people the knowledge of salvation through the forgiveness of their sins,	
⁷⁸because of the tender mercy of our God, by which the rising sun will come to us from heaven	

Zechariah's Song	Old Testament References
79to shine on those living in darkness and in the shadow of death, to guide our feet into the path of peace.	But for you who revere my name, the sun of righteousness will rise with healing in its wings. And you will go out and leap like calves released from the stall. *Malachi 4:2* The people walking in darkness have seen a great light; on those living in the land of the shadow of death a light has dawned. *Isaiah 9:2* Then your light will break forth like the dawn, and your healing will quickly appear; then your righteousness will go before you, and the glory of the LORD will be your rear guard. *Isaiah 58:8* "Arise, shine, for your light has come, and the glory of the LORD rises upon you. See, darkness covers the earth and thick darkness is over the peoples, but the LORD rises upon you and his glory appears over you. *Isaiah 60:1-2*

Carol Lines to Hymn

Song of the Angels
(Gloria in Excelsis Deo)

Luke 2:13-14
(New International Version [NIV])
Suddenly a great company of the heavenly host appeared with the angel, praising God and saying, "Glory to God in the highest, and on earth peace to men on whom his favor rests."

This is undoubtedly the most famous of the Christmas songs. It certainly is the shortest in this series. These words have formed the basis of numerous carols through the years. The angels' song has been used as a refrain for carols as well as found their way inside carols we hear and sing every Christmas season.

And what a glorious song this must have been! The angels are given but few chances to share the Gospel. This was one of them. I can picture that this song was likely the most beautiful ever heard in earth's history. I wonder if anyone in Bethlehem, or even Jerusalem five miles to the north, heard the song as it was sung? Or was that honor granted to the shepherds alone?

Whenever an angel appears in Scripture, it signifies a significant episode in salvation history. The first angels to appear in Scripture's pages are the seraphim who guarded the Garden of Eden. This would have prevented Adam and Eve from eating of the tree of life. Eating of the tree would have doomed mankind to an eternity of "life" in sin's domination. Imagine all the ailments that we suffer, which increase with age, being a part of us for all eternity (and time also being a part of existence). The posting of the angel guards was necessary so that death would give us respite from sin's ills—and a Savior could come to die in our place to pay for sin.

Angels appeared with the pre-incarnate God to Abraham to announce the birth of Isaac. Angels appeared to Isaiah at the beginning of his ministry. Angels announce to Zechariah and to Mary their life-altering pregnancies. An angel appears to Joseph in dreams to convince him to remain with Mary and later to escape to Egypt when Herod ordered the execution of babies. Angels appear at the Resurrection and also at the Ascension. These rare occurrences were given the angels to proclaim God's love and mercy.

And these angels give glory to God, the one who sits "in the highest." No Caesar can usurp this God. Everything which Luke records previously about Jesus birth, and the government decree it took to get Jesus to be born in Bethlehem, were because the God in the highest orders His creation and controls world events.

Yes, the angels proclaim peace, but what peace did they proclaim? Obviously not world peace, because the world is still at war. At any one time there is a conflict, if not several, somewhere in the world. People also do not have peace in their souls. Demons and spirits of many types occupy their hearts, souls, and minds. They find no peace even as they sink deeper into their demons and spirits seeking that peace.

But the Prince of Peace brings peace, but not peace between political entities or even between individuals. In Matthew he speaks of the end times marked by warfare and the strife faith in him would cause among families. But Jesus brings peace between God and man by serving as an atonement for sin. Sin has been taken away as a barrier between God and man, taken away by the death and resurrection of Jesus Christ! And because Jesus has taken away this barrier, you and I are now among those on whom his favor rests. We have been redeemed! We are now children of the king, with an eternal inheritance!

And having such a great treasure, as we learn more and more about this treasure and the love behind it, the more and more God dispels the demons and spirits in our lives and fills our lives with His Spirit.

May the joy of the Angels' Song fill your heart with joy not only this Yuletide, but throughout the coming year.

Carol Lines to Hymn

Song of Simeon
(Nunc Dimittis)

Luke 2:28-32
(New International Version [NIV])

Simeon took him in his arms and praised God, saying:
   "Sovereign Lord, as you have promised,
   you now dismiss your servant in peace.
   For my eyes have seen your salvation,
   which you have prepared in the sight of all people,
   a light for revelation to the Gentiles
   and for glory to your people Israel."

In this song we meet a temple worker named Simeon. He was promised by God that he wouldn't see death before seeing the fulfillment of the Promise, the coming of the Messiah.

And this meeting takes place when Jesus is eight days old. In accordance with the Law Jesus was consecrated at the temple. This rite basically hearkens back to the Passover night in Egypt, when God struck the firstborn in the Land of Egypt. Only those who painted the blood of a lamb on their doorposts were spared by the angel of death. In recognition of this, God demanded that the firstborn be consecrated to Him.

But he didn't want child sacrifices, as the Canaanites practiced. Rather, he decreed that a bull, or two doves, be sacrificed in their place.

A woman who had given birth also had to be ceremonially purified before she could partake of the temple rites as well. Thus Mary and Joseph travel five miles from Bethlehem to Jerusalem to consecrate Jesus with the offering of two doves and the purification of Mary. And Simeon, waiting for the fulfillment, sees the Messiah and knows who this one special child is.

No doubt Simeon had inside information. I'm sure he worked with Zechariah, a priest, and knew the miraculous circumstances of the birth of John six months previous. And Mary herself had stayed with Zechariah and Elizabeth for several months. Simeon and Mary had to have crossed paths at some point—or at the very least he knew the time was near. Even if Zechariah couldn't speak, Elizabeth was still free of tongue.

Simeon also includes Gentiles in his song! Later, in Jesus' ministry, the court of the Gentiles would be the site of the moneychangers who did temple business. No doubt the reason for the Court of the Gentiles was lost on the Jewish leaders. But Simeon understood, and knew that this Messiah was sent for all people, not just Israel.

The Latin title, *Nunc Dimittis*, simply means "dismiss now." In a sense, Simeon is saying, "May I be dismissed now? I have seen that my salvation is here!"

Simeon refers to Isaiah's prophecy in his song, as seen in the following table.

Simeon's Song	Old Testament Reference
[29]Sovereign Lord, as you have promised, you now dismiss your servant in peace.	
[30]For my eyes have seen your salvation,	And the glory of the LORD will be revealed, and all mankind together will see it. For the mouth of the LORD has spoken. *Isaiah 40:5*
[31]which you have prepared in the sight of all people,	The LORD will lay bare his holy arm in the sight of all the nations, and all the ends of the earth will see the salvation of our God. *Isaiah 52:10*
[32]a light for revelation to the Gentiles	"I, the LORD, have called you in righteousness; I will take hold of your hand. I will keep you and will make you to be a covenant for the people and a light for the Gentiles, *Isaiah 42:6* "It is too small a thing for you to be my servant to restore the tribes of Jacob and bring back those of Israel I have kept. I will also make you a light for the Gentiles, that you may bring my salvation to the ends of the earth." *Isaiah 49:6*
and for glory to your people Israel.	I am bringing my righteousness near, it is not far away; and my salvation will not be delayed. I will grant salvation to Zion, my splendor to Israel. *Isaiah 46:13*

Ancient Hymns

Carol Lines to Hymn

Of The Father's Love Begotten

"Of The Father's Love Begotten" is a hymn that comes down to us from Prudentius in the 5th Century. Christians have been singing it for over 1500 years.

Aurelius Clemens Prudentius was born in 348AD in Spain. A Christian Latin poet, Prudentius wrote a number of hymns, occasional Christian lyrics, and poems on saints. Although he held a high place at the Roman court, he eventually retired to devote himself to religion.

Prudentius has been called "the father of Christian allegory." Prudentius achieved distinction in government administration but retired in later life to write devotional poetry, becoming the first to use the classical Latin verse forms with complete success in the service of the new faith. His lyrical poetry includes "Hymns for the Day," a cycle of twelve hymns for various times of the day, parts of which are still found in modern hymnals; and "Crowns of Martyrdom," fourteen long poems celebrating the lives of martyrs, including "The Passion of Agnes." Prudentius also wrote two long didactic poems: *Apotheosis*, on the doctrine of the Trinity; and *Hamartigenia* (*Origin of Sin*), which attacks the Gnostic theologian Marcion. Other works include *Psychomachia*, an allegorical description of the struggle between (Christian) virtues and (pagan) vices; *Contra Symmachum*, a polemic against paganism based on the events of the year 384; and a series of 49 poems describing biblical scenes depicted in wall paintings on a Roman church—a valuable source on Christian iconography.

The date of the hymn's writing, though not entirely known, can be deduced through the life of Prudentius. Prudentius would have lived at the time of the Arian heresy and the Council at Nicea. The hymn reflects many of the statements set out in the Athanasian Creed.

A look at the theology of this hymn reflects the unique nature of Christ as reflected in this hymn.

The hymn has become a standard Christmas hymn in the church, usually in association with John 1:1-18.

"Of the Father's Love Begotten"
by Aurelius C. Prudentius, 413, cento
Translated by John. M. Neale, 1818-1866
and Henry W. Baker, 1821-1977

1. Of the Father's love begotten
   Ere the worlds began to be,
   He is Alpha and Omega,
   He the Source, the Ending He,
   Of the things that are, that have been,
   And that future years shall see
   Evermore and evermore.

The hymn starts straight off on why a small baby was born in Bethlehem. There was a cosmic quality to this birth, an eternal element, an ingredient that defies reason and logic. "Of the Father's love begotten." God so love the world that he gave his one and only Son that whoever believes in him should not perish but have everlasting life (John 3:16). And this begetting occurred before the world was created! The joyful message of Christmas is this: God knew what all people would do before he created the world and us people in it. He knew what each of us would do before he created each one of us. Yet he still created the world, and he still sent His Son to die for us. No matter what you did, you are forgiven through the blood of Christ.

Prudentius reminds us of the words spoken to John in his Revelation: Jesus is the Alpha and Omega. Jesus was there at the earth's creation. You know what that means? Jesus was in consultation with his Father in creating the people who would rebel! Jesus knew, creating those people, that he would have to die to pay for their sins! And in creating the human body he would be building in the anatomy that would cause him excruciating pain on the cross.

And in the end, Jesus will be ruling, just as he rules now from on high.

2. Oh, that birth forever blessed
When the Virgin, full of grace,
By the Holy Ghost conceiving,
Bare the Savior of our race,
And the Babe, the world's Redeemer,
First revealed His sacred face
Evermore and evermore.

Prudentius now takes us to that manger in Bethlehem. Look, the virgin has conceived and has given birth—and has called him name Immanuel ("God with us")!

Notice how Prudentius describes Mary? "Full of grace." It was by grace that Mary was chosen to be the vessel of God, not because she was sinless. In her "Magnificat," Mary states her sinful condition when she states "because of God my Savior." She states her need of a Savior and, paradoxically, that she is bearing and giving birth to that Savior!

3. O ye heights of heaven, adore Him;
Angel hosts, His praises sing;
Powers, dominions, bow before Him
And extol our God and King.
Let no tongue on earth be silent,
Every voice in concert ring
Evermore and evermore.

Can't you just see that angelic choir singing above Judea's hillsides to the shepherds? Prudentius sums up that scene eloquently in this verse, stating the totality of the heavenly chorus.

And, of course, the shepherds couldn't keep this news to themselves. They rushed to see the baby, then rushed to announce the joyous news. No doubt the citizens of Bethlehem were all astir on that night so long ago, the Roman legions standing guard on alert. Just what were they to make of this spectacle?

4. This is He whom Heaven-taught singers
   Sang of old with one accord;
   Whom the Scriptures of the prophets
   Promised in their faithful word.
   Now He shines, the Long-expected;
   Let creation praise its Lord
   Evermore and evermore.

Lest we think the angels were out of place, Prudentius tells us that the angels stated the fulfillment of Old Testament prophets. Taking a cue from St. Paul ("If anyone, even an angel, speaks a Gospel different than the Gospel I proclaimed to you, let him be condemned" Galatians 1:8), Prudentius points out the angelic message's harmony with Old Testament prophesy.

5. Christ, to Thee, with God the Father,
   And, O Holy Ghost, to Thee
   Hymn and chant and high thanksgiving
   And unending praises be,
   Honor, glory, and dominion,
   And eternal victory
   Evermore and evermore.

Prudentius finishes (in this English version found in *The Lutheran Hymnal*) with a Trinitarian doxology, common among early Christians. It reasserts the truths of the Trinity stated in the Athanasian Creed as well as the honor

45

due the Triune God, which includes the Son of God, the baby lying in Bethlehem's manger.

Source of lyrics:
> *The Lutheran Hymnal*
> Hymn #98
> Text: 1 Tim. 3:16
> Author: Aurelius C. Prudentius, 413, cento
> Translated by: John. M. Neale, 1854 and Henry W. Baker, 1861
> Titled: "Corde natus ex Parentis"
> Tune: "Divinum mysterium", Plain-song tune, 12th century

The original Latin, for all you Latin scholars:

Corde natus ex parentis

1. corde natus ex parentis
   ante mundi exordium
   A et O cognominatus,
   ipse fons et clausula
   omnium quae sunt, fuerunt,
   quaeque post futura sunt.

2. Ipse iussit et creata,
   dixit ipse et facta sunt,
   terra, caelum, fossa ponti,
   trina rerum machina,
   quaeque in his vigent sub alto
   solis et lunae globo.

3. Corporis formam caduci,
   membra morti obnoxia
   induit, ne gens periret
   primoplasti ex germine,
   merserat quem lex profundo
   noxialis tartaro.

4. O beatus ortus ille,
   virgo cum puerperal
   edidit nostram salutem,
   feta Sancto Spiritu,
   et puer redemptor orbis
   os sacratum protulit.

5. Psallat altitudo caeli,
   psallite omnes angeli,
   quidquid est virtutis usquam
   psallat in laudem Dei,
   nulla linguarum silescat,
   vox et omnis consonet.

6. Ecce, quem vates vetustis
   concinebant saeculis,
   quem prophetarum fideles
   paginae spoponderant,
   emicat promissus olim;
   cuncta conlaudent eum.

7. Macte iudex mortuorum,
   macte rex viventium,
   dexter in Parentis arce
   qui cluis virtutibus,
   omnium venturus inde
   iustus ultor criminum.

8. Te senes et te iuventus,
   parvulorum te chorus,
   turba matrum, virginumque,
   simplices puellulae,
   voce concordes pudicis
   perstrepant concentibus.

9. Tibi, Christe, sit cum Patre
   hagioque Pneumate
   hymnus, decus, laus perennis,
   gratiarum actio,
   honor, virtus, victoria,
   regnum aeternaliter.

Songs of Thankfulness and Praise

This hymn is often associated with the Christmas season
(Epiphany, actually), not necessarily Thanksgiving. But
then, in American culture Thanksgiving has traditionally
kicked off the "unofficial" Christmas season (as far as
merchants used to be concerned; now Christmas items are
already edging out the Hallowe'en candy in mid-October).
In the church, the Sunday after Thanksgiving is often the
First Sunday of Advent, the start of the Christmas cycle of
a new Church Year.

The hymn was written by Christopher Wordsworth in 1862.
Christopher Wordsworth was born 30 October 1807 in
Bocking, Essex, England. Christopher was the nephew of
poet William Wordsworth. Christopher was both a scholar
and athlete in his student days and later served as
headmaster of Harrow Boys School from 1836 to 1850.
(Winston Churchill would attend this same school a
century later.)

Wordsworth was also vicar at Stanford-in-the-Vale, Berkshire, from 1850 to 1869 and the archdeacon of Westminster. He became a bishop of Lincoln in 1868. Wordsworth, as befitting his name, was a recognized Greek scholar who also wrote theological and other works. Wordsworth said of his hymns: "It is the first duty of a hymn to teach sound doctrine and thence to save souls."

Wordsworth's books include:
- *Athens and Attica* (1836),
- *Ancient Writings Copied from the Walls of Pompeii* (1837),
- *Greece, Pictoral, Descriptive, and Historical* (1839),
- *Theophilus Anglicanus* (1843),
- *On the Canon of the Scriptures* (1848),
- *Memoirs of William Wordsworth* (1851),
- *Commentary on the Whole Bible* (1856-70),
- *The Holy Year; or Hymns for Sundays and Holydays throughout the Year, And for other Occasions* (1863), and
- *Church History*, 1881-83

Wordsworth's hymns include
- "Arm These Thy Soldiers, Mighty Lord,"
- "The Day Is Gently Sinking to a Close,"
- "Father of All, from Land and Sea,"
- "Gracious Spirit, Holy Ghost,"
- "The Grave Itself a Garden Is,"
- "Hallelujah! Christ Is Risen,"
- "Hark! the Sound of Holy Voices,"
- "Hearts to Heaven and Voices Raise,"
- "Heav'nly Father, Send Thy Blessing,"
- "Holy, Holy, Holy Lord,"
- "Lord, Be Thy Word My Rule,"

- "O Day of Rest and Gladness,"
- "O Lord, Our Strength in Weakness,"
- "See, the Conqueror Mounts in Triumph,"
- "Sing, O Sing, This Blessed Morn," and
- "Songs of Thankfulness and Praise."

Wordsworth died on 20 March 1885 in Lincoln, England, and was buried in the graveyard of the church at Riseholme College, north of Lincoln.

Hymn Text From:
The Lutheran Hymnal
(St. Louis: Concordia Publishing House, 1941)

1. Songs of thankfulness and praise,
   Jesus, Lord, to Thee we raise,
   Manifested by the star
   To the sages from afar,
   Branch of royal David's stem,
   In Thy birth at Bethlehem.
   Anthems be to Thee addressed
   God in man made manifest.

The first verse begins with what we consider the final
chapter in the infant Jesus' cycle of his life-the visit by the
Magi. The hymn writer notes the supernatural qualities of
Jesus and his birth-the star's appearance, sages visiting,
Jesus' lineage from King David, the birth at Bethlehem.
These were all marks of the Messiah that God promised
from ancient days to His people.

2. Manifest at Jordan's stream,
   Prophet, Priest, and King supreme,
   And at Cana, Wedding-guest,
   In Thy Godhead manifest;
   Manifest in power divine,
   Changing water into wine.
   Anthems be to Thee addressed
   God in man made manifest.

Next the hymn writer shows the beginning of the ministry
of Jesus. The two events highlighted are the baptism of
Jesus by John the Baptizer and the wedding at Cana where
Jesus performed his first miracle. That miracle turned

water into wine. The author also relates the three offices of Jesus: prophet, priest, and king. As prophet, Jesus is the Word who speaks for God. As priest Jesus offered himself as the sacrifice for all our sin. As king, Jesus rules both in our hearts as our faith is created and strengthened and in world events until the Father declares the times are fulfilled.

> 3. Manifest in making whole
> Manifest in valiant fight,
> Quelling all the devil's might;
> Manifest in gracious will,
> Ever bringing good from ill.
> Anthems be to Thee addressed,
> God in man made manifest.

"In all things God works good for those that love Him," St. Paul wrote to the Roman congregation. The hymn writer echoes that sentiment with this verse. It relates what Jesus' ministry became known for among his contemporaries-he healed the sick, made the blind see and the lame walk, and raised the dead.

> 4. Sun and moon shall darkened be,
> Stars shall fall, the heavens shall flee;
> Christ will then like lightning shine,
> All will see His glorious sign;
> All will then the trumpet hear,
> All will see the Judge appear;
> Thou by all wilt be confessed,
> God in man made manifest.

The hymn writer goes on to speak of the Judgment Day. And the words convey joy, not trepidation! And Christians should look forward to the Judgment Day with joy and thanksgiving! For then we will go home to be with our Lord and Savior for all eternity. Allelujah!

5. Grant us grace to see Thee, Lord,
   Mirrored in Thy holy Word;
   May we imitate Thee now
   And be pure as pure art Thou
   That we like to Thee may be
   At Thy great Epiphany
   And may praise Thee, ever blest,
   God in man made manifest.

The hymn writer concludes with a prayer-a prayer that we continue in His Word and see our image becoming more like our heavenly Father's image. The perfection will be made complete at "they great Epiphany." I take this to mean the Judgment when Jesus will be manifest to all people as the Lord and Savior and Judge. In faith we know that our judgment is rendered moot.

The word "Epiphany" means "to make manifest." As you likely noticed, each verse echoes this word's theme: "God in man made manifest." Jesus is the God-man who manifested himself here on earth and will be manifested to all on Judgment.

Notes:

Hymn #134 from *The Lutheran Hymnal*
Hymn # 88 from *Lutheran Worship*

Text: 1 Peter 1:20: "He was chosen before the creation of the world, but was revealed in these last times for your sake."

Author: Christopher Wordsworth, 1862
Composer: George J. Elvey, 1858
Tune: "St. George"
Alternate setting: Music: Salzburg melody Jakob Hintze
(17th C) harm. J. S. Bach (18th C)

Carol Lines to Hymn

From Heaven Above to Earth I Come

Hymn 85 from *The Lutheran Hymnal*
Text: Luke 2: 1-18
Author: Martin Luther, 1535
Tune: "Vom Himmel hoch, da komm' ich her"
Translated by: Catherine Winkworth, 1855, alt.
1st published in: *Geistliche Lieder*
Leipzig, 1539

Luther had a little tradition with his household (likely included students who couldn't make it to their homes for Christmas). This hymn he wrote would be sung in two parts; the first verses sung by someone dressed like an angel and descending a staircase, while the last verses were sung by the assemble household members at the bottom of the staircase.

Luther had a childlike appreciation for Christmas. Read Roland Bainton's *Luther's Christmas Book* for more on Luther and Christmas.

The "angel" sang:

1. "From heaven above to earth I come
   To bear good news to every home;
   Glad tidings of great joy I bring,
   Whereof I now will say and sing:

2. "To you this night is born a child
   Of Mary, chosen virgin mild;
   This little child, of lowly birth,
   Shall be the joy of all the earth.

3. "This is the Christ, our God and Lord,
   Who in all need shall aid afford;
   He will Himself your Savior be
   From all your sins to set you free.

4. "He will on you the gifts bestow
   Prepared by God for all below,
   That in His kingdom, bright and fair,
   You may with us His glory share.

5. "These are the tokens ye shall mark:
   The swaddling-clothes and manger dark;
   There ye shall find the Infant laid
   By whom the heavens and earth were made."

The assembly would sing:

6. Now let us all with gladsome cheer
   Go with the shepherds and draw near
   To see the precious gift of God,
   Who hath His own dear Son bestowed.

7. Give heed, my heart, lift up thine eyes!
   What is it in yon manger lies?
   Who is this child, so young and fair?
   The blessed Christ-child lieth there.

8. Welcome to earth, Thou noble Guest,
   Through whom the sinful world is blest!
   Thou com'st to share my misery;
   What thanks shall I return to Thee?

9. Ah, Lord, who hast created all,
   How weak art Thou, how poor and small,
   That Thou dost choose Thine infant bed
   Where humble cattle lately fed!

10. Were earth a thousand times as fair,
    Beset with gold and jewels rare,
    It yet were far too poor to be
    A narrow cradle, Lord, for Thee.

11. For velvets soft and silken stuff
    Thou hast but hay and straw so rough,
    Whereon Thou, King, so rich and great,
    As 'twere Thy heaven, art throned in state.

12. And thus, dear Lord, it pleaseth Thee
    To make this truth quite plain to me,
    That all the world's wealth, honor, might,
    Are naught and worthless in Thy sight.

13. Ah, dearest Jesus, holy Child,
    Make Thee a bed, soft, undefiled,
    Within my heart, that it may be
    A quiet chamber kept for Thee.

14. My heart for very joy doth leap,
    My lips no more can silence keep;
    I, too, must sing with joyful tongue
    That sweetest ancient cradle-song:

15. Glory to God in highest heaven,
    Who unto us His Son hath given!
    While angels sing with pious mirth
    A glad new year to all the earth.

Jesu, Joy of Man's Desiring

Composer: Johann Sebastian Bach (Germany, 1685-1750)

Written: First draft December 1716, first performance 2 July 1723

Title: Cantata No. 147 (BWV 147), "Herz und Mund und Tat und Leben", No. 10: "Jesu bleibet meine Freunde"

What it is: The final choral section from one of Bach's 200-plus cantatas

Length: 3'30" (complete cantata 25')

Why it's famous: The lilting serenity of the tune became
familiar from Myra Hess's 1920s transcription for
piano, when it gained its English title
Where you heard it before: The Beach Boys' "Lady
Linda;" Ralph McTell's "Dreams of You;" in TV ads
and films; at a wedding somewhere.

A recent poll on this topic found as the overwhelming
favorite composition of Johann Sebastian Bach to be "Jesu,
Joy of Man's Desiring." "Jesu Joy of Man's Desiring"
(German: "Jesu, bleibet meine Freude"), was originally
composed for trumpet, oboe, strings, and organ. The piece
is perhaps best known in an arrangement written by
British pianist Dame Myra Hess (1890-1965). Why was
"Jesu, Joy of Man's Desiring" written and what was Bach's
inspiration for writing this inspirational piece?

Today, a composer who can write excellent music to order
makes a very lucrative living churning out film scores. In
the 1700s the same talent would have been put to work
writing music for church services, which gobbled up music
at the rate of a big half-hour or hour work every Sunday or
so. Needless to say, it didn't pay all that well.

As the director of church music in Leipzig in the 1720s,
Bach had to supply endless cantatas. A cantata is a setting
of religious words for choir and instruments.

Bach usually started on Monday. The composing and
copying of all the instrumental parts took four days
(Monday through Thursday). First rehearsals were on
Friday, dress rehearsals on Saturday, performance at 8am
on Sunday.

Bach did four complete cycles of 52 weeks like this, possibly more. Though there's often a bit of judicious recycling and reuse here and there, and a few sections of padding, Bach's cantatas are an incredible collection of great music that have attracted many great musical minds. One such was Myra Hess, who liked this theme so much she transcribed it for piano. Something about its lilting serenity appealed to a wide audience, and made it a hit with the listener in the street. It has since appeared in the background of many TV ads and films.

So next time you feel pressured at work, spare a thought for old Johann Sebastian. "Jesu, Joy of Man's Desiring" is a three-minute extract from a thirty-minute cantata. That cantata is just one of over 200 that survived. Those 200 cantatas form only a fifth of Bach's works as listed in the BWV catalogue. And those thousand-odd works are only a fraction of what survived. In other words, "Jesu" represents less than 0.01% of his output. Clearly his employers kept him pretty busy.

Many today perform "Jesu, Joy of Man's Desiring." Often you find it as part of a Christmas collection (and, quite frankly, makes for a better Christmas song than Julia Andrews, "Favorite Things" from *The Sound of Music*). Some of my favorite recordings are Amy Grant's rendition on her second Christmas CD, Rebecca St. James who gives Bach's piece an edge to it, and the piece in its original German in *The Sacred Cantatas: Famous Chorus*.

This piece is also a favorite at weddings. No doubt the joyous, upbeat movements are a nice addition to the service. It has even been adapted for use in several Celtic musical anthologies!

German Lyrics

Jesus, des Menschen Freude.
Du, dessen Liebe wie eine Laterne herabscheint,
zu Dir hingezogen werden die Seelen, die Dir entgegen streben.
Durch unseren Glauben erreichen wir eine himmlische Höhe.
Sohn Gottes, wir beten, daß wir Dich erreichen,
mögen wir in Frieden leben, wir flehen Dich an. Öffne Türen der
unbekannten Wahrheit,
wie Deine Liebe herab kommt vom himmlischen Thron,
lehre uns von Deinem himmlischen Thron (aus). Öffne Türen der
unbekannten Wahrheit,
wie Deine Liebe herab kommt vom himmlischen Thron.

English Lyrics

Jesu, joy of man's desiring, Holy wisdom, love most bright;
Drawn by Thee, our souls aspiring Soar to uncreated light.
Word of God, our flesh that fashioned, With the fire of life
impassioned,
Striving still to truth unknown,
Soaring, dying round Thy throne. Through the way where hope
is guiding,
Hark, what peaceful music rings; Where the flock, in Thee
confiding,
Drink of joy from deathless springs. Theirs is beauty's fairest
pleasure;
Theirs is wisdom's holiest treasure. Thou dost ever lead Thine
own In the love of joys unknown.

Hark the Herald Angels Sing

The next chapter looks at the life of composer Felix Mendelssohn and his contributions not only to music but church music as well. The tune for "Hark! The Herald Angels Sing" was from Mendelssohn's own repertoire. But how the tune came to be married to the carol is another story. And on top of this story is the story of how we got "Hark! The Herald Angels Sing."

"Hark! The Herald Angels Sing" was written by Charles Wesley in 1737. Originally he called it "Hark, how all the welkin rings, Glory to the King of Kings!" *Welkin* is an old English word that means "heaven," "sky," or "the vaults of heaven."

The words we have today came from George Whitefield, an old college friend of Wesley's. Friendship, however, has its limits. Wesley did not like the change in lyrics. It was his contention that the Scriptures do not speak of angels singing in Luke's account (although the King James

Version does have "a multitude of the heavenly host," unless Wesley believed there were more entities than angels in that heavenly choir). The carol hymn was popular before; it became even more popular with the change. Wesley steadfastly refused to sing the new words, although that's fair. He did write the carol hymn, after all.

But Mendelssohn's tune still wasn't part of the "Hark!" hymn originally. I haven't found anyone anywhere who knows what the actual tune (or tunes) originally sung with this hymn were. Whatever tune or tunes were used became lost in the mists of history as Mendelssohn's tune became the popular tune fixed in the public's mind.

The tune used, named "Mendelssohn," was not originally intended for any Christmas carol or hymn, much less this one. In fact it wasn't intended for church use. In 1855 William Cummings took Mendelssohn's "Festgesang an die Knüstler" ("Festival song at the Knustler") and matched it up with Whitefield's words. "Festgesang" was a tribute to Johann Gutenberg and his invention of the movable type printing press. Today this combination is considered a Christmas classic and featured in almost all hymnals and a majority of Christmas albums.

Geo. Whitefield's words	Charles Wesley's words
Hark! The herald angels sing, "Glory to the newborn King; Peace on earth, and mercy mild, God and sinners reconciled!"	Hark, how all the welkin rings, "Glory to the King of kings; Peace on earth, and mercy mild, God and sinners reconciled!"
Joyful, all ye nations rise, Join the triumph of the skies; With th'angelic host proclaim, "Christ is born in Bethlehem!" (Refrain)	Joyful, all ye nations, rise, Join the triumph of the skies; Universal nature say, "Christ the Lord is born today!"

Geo. Whitefield's words	Charles Wesley's words
Refrain *Hark! the herald angels sing,* *"Glory to the newborn King!"*	
Christ, by highest heav'n adored; Christ the everlasting Lord; Late in time, behold Him come, Offspring of a virgin's womb. Veiled in flesh the Godhead see; Hail th'incarnate Deity, Pleased with us in flesh to dwell, Jesus our Emmanuel. (Refrain)	Christ, by highest Heaven ador'd, Christ, the everlasting Lord: Late in time behold him come, Offspring of a Virgin's womb!
	Veiled in flesh, the Godhead see, Hail the incarnate deity! Pleased as man with men to appear, Jesus! Our Immanuel here!
Hail the heav'nly Prince of Peace! Hail the Sun of Righteousness! Light and life to all He brings, Ris'n with healing in His wings. Mild He lays His glory by,	Hail, the heavenly Prince of Peace! Hail, the Sun of Righteousness! Light and life to all he brings, Risen with healing in his wings.
Born that man no more may die. Born to raise the sons of earth, Born to give them second birth. (Refrain)	Mild He lays his glory by, Born that man no more may die; Born to raise the sons of earth; Born to give them second birth.

Come, Desire of nations, come,
Fix in us Thy humble home;
Rise, the woman's conqu'ring
    Seed,
Bruise in us the serpent's head.
	Come, Desire of nations, come,
	Fix in us thy humble home;
	Rise, the woman's conquering
	    seed,
	Bruise in us the serpent's head.

Now display Thy saving power, Ruined nature now restore; Now in mystic union join Thine to ours, and ours to Thine. (Refrain)	Now display thy saving power, Ruined nature now restore; Now in mystic union join Thine to ours, and ours to thine.
Adam's likeness, Lord, efface, Stamp Thine image in its place: Second Adam from above, Reinstate us in Thy love.	Adam's likeness, Lord, efface; Stamp Thy image in its place. Second Adam from above, Reinstate us in thy love.
Let us Thee, though lost, regain, Thee, the Life, the inner man: O, to all Thyself impart, Formed in each believing heart. (Refrain)	Let us Thee, though lost, regain, Thee, the life, the inner Man: O! to all thyself impart, Form'd in each believing heart.

Note: I'm not sure when the refrain was added—whether it was added by George Whitefield or added to fit Mendelssohn's tune.

Resources used:

Stories Behind the Best-Loved Songs of Christmas by Ace Collins (2004, Running Press Book Publishers)

101 More Hymn Stories by Kenneth W. Osbeck (1985, Kregel Publications)

Hark! Felix Mendelssohn Compose

In Lutheran and musical circles, Johann Sebastian Bach is revered as a gifted musician. He is known as the "theologian of music" for the pieces he wrote for the church. Yet Bach for many years was forgotten as a musician. Bach was a composer of the Baroque style when Baroque was waning in popularity. It is likely Bach was seen as "old fashioned" by his contemporaries.

It would be after his death that Bach would gain renown for his music and become a giant among composers. And for this renewed popularity Bach owes a debt of gratitude to another Lutheran composer, the German composer Felix Jakob Ludwig Mendelssohn-Bartholdy, commonly known as Felix Mendelssohn.

On 11 March 1829, Mendelssohn conducted the "St. Matthew Passion," stimulating a revival of interest in the music of J. S. Bach. This was 79 years after Bach had died! The public reception of this piece was so overwhelming that

Bach's music was once again popular in the mainstream. Mendelssohn led the revival of the music of Bach.

Mendelssohn was by birth Jewish and the grandson of the Jewish philosopher Moses Mendelssohn. Felix's father, Abraham, converted to Christianity in 1816 and changed his surname to Mendelssohn-Bartholdy.

Mendelssohn was born in Hamburg on 3 February 1809. His family were bankers in Berlin and thus Mendelssohn grew up privileged. Mendelssohn studied the piano with Ludwig Berger and theory and composition with Karl Friedrich Zelter. He produced his first piece in 1820 at the age of 11. Mendelssohn's early influences included the poetry of Goethe (whom he knew from 1821) and the Schlegel translations of Shakespeare. These influences are traceable in Mendelssohn's best music of the period, including the exuberant "String Octet op.20" and the vivid, poetic overture to *A Midsummer Night's Dream.*

A period of travel and concert-giving introduced Mendelssohn to England, Scotland (1829), and Italy (1830-31). Mendelssohn made return visits to Paris (1831) and London (1832, 1833) before he took up a conducting post at Düsseldorf (1833-5). In Düsseldorf Mendelssohn concentrated on Handel's oratorios. Among the chief products of this time were *The Hebrides* (first performed in London in 1832), the "g Minor Piano Concerto," Die erste Walpurgisnacht, the Italian Symphony (1833, London) and St. Paul (1836, Düsseldorf).

Mendelssohn became a conductor and music organizer in Leipzig in 1835, where he served until 1847. Here to great acclaim he conducted the Gewandhaus Orchestra, championing both historical and modern works of Bach,

Beethoven, Weber, Schumann, Berlioz. Mendelssohn also founded and directed the Leipzig Conservatory in 1843.

Mendelssohn composed mostly in the summer holidays. He produced Ruy Blas, revised the Hymn of Praise, the "Scottish Symphony," and the now famous "Violin Concerto op.64." Meanwhile, he was intermittently employed by the king as a composer and choirmaster in Berlin, where he wrote highly successful incidental music, notably for *A Midsummer Night's Dream* (1843). Much sought after as a festival organizer, he was associated especially with the Lower Rhine and Birmingham music festivals.
Mendelssohn paid ten visits to England, the last two (1840-7) to conduct Elijah in Birmingham and London.
Always a warm friend and valued colleague, he was devoted to his family.

Mendelssohn died in Leipzig on 4 November 1847 at the age of 38, after a series of strokes. He was mourned internationally. Lutherans also owe a debt of gratitude for making Bach's music come alive again. During this Christmas season we can also be thankful for another tune Mendelssohn wrote: "Hark! The Herald Angels Sing."

Mendelssohn also wrote a harmony to the hymn written by a Lutheran pastor, "Now Thank We All Our God." Though his life was short, Felix Mendelssohn contributed with his talents and abilities in God's Kingdom.

Carol Lines to Hymn

Modern Praises

Carol Lines to Hymn

Now the Silence/
Then the Glory

"Now the Silence,"
Christian Worship: A Lutheran Hymnal, #231
"Then the Glory,"
Christian Worship: A Lutheran Hymnal, #218

A favorite Christmas CD of mine was issued by Concordia Publishing House and called *The Marvel of This Night.* This CD featured the Christmas hymns of a hymn writer named Jaroslav Vajda. Several of his hymns have made their way into *Christian Worship: A Lutheran Hymnal* and *Let All the People Praise You,* a spiritual songbook published by the Wisconsin Evangelical Lutheran Synod and Northwestern Publishing House. In this section I share several of Vajda's hymns this Advent and Christmas season and some thoughts on these hymns.

Jaroslav Vajda is the son of a Lutheran pastor of Slovak descent who received musical training in childhood. Vajda began translating classical Slovak poetry at age eighteen but did not write his first hymn until age 49. He has written over 200 original and translated hymns, which appear worldwide in more than 65 hymnals. He also published two collections of hymn texts, numerous books, translations, and articles. Vajda served on hymnal commissions for *Hymnal Supplement* (1969) and *Lutheran Book of Worship* (1978). After 18 years in a mostly bilingual ministry, he became the editor of *This Day* Magazine and then became a book editor and developer at Concordia Publishing House. Jaroslav Vajda retired in 1986.

The two hymns featured here are short—each is one verse long. Technically they are not Christmas hymns. "Now the Silence" is placed in the "Opening of Service" section of *Christian Worship.* "Then the Glory" is in the "End Time" section. "Now the Silence," however, brings us into that silent, reverent mood-indeed, a mood fit to meet the baby king who created each one of us. A focus on Advent is the coming of our Savior to judge the world and gather his saints to heaven. Thus "Then the Glory" fits this aspect of our Advent meditation.

Both hymns use the tune "Now," which was composed by Carl F. Schalk. Vajda's hymns are often set to Schalk's compositions.

Carl Flentge Schalk was born in Chicago in 1929. He earned a B.S. in Ed. from Concordia College, River Forest, Illinois, and advanced degrees from the Eastman School of Music, Rochester , N.Y., (M.Mus) and Concordia Seminary, St. Louis (M.A.R.). Schalk is a Distinguished Professor of Music Emeritus at Concordia University, in River Forest,

Illinois, where he taught graduate courses in church music since 1965. He served in the parish as a teacher and director of music at Zion Lutheran Church in Wausau, Wisconsin. He served the church-at-large as the director of music for the International Lutheran Hour, as the editor of the journal Church Music from 1966-1980, and served on various boards and committees for The Hymn Society, the National Association of Pastoral Musicians, and the Inter-Lutheran Commission on Worship (ILCW). The ILCW prepared the *Lutheran Book of Worship* and developed a new periscope reading schedule. His choral compositions and hymn settings for congregational use are widely used and he has written over 50 hymn tunes and carols.

Now the Silence
> *Now the silence*
> *Now the peace*
> *Now the empty hands uplifted*
> *Now the kneeling*
> *Now the plea*
> *Now the Father's arms in welcome*
> *Now the hearing*
> *Now the pow'r*
> *Now the vessel brimmed for pouring*
> *Now the body*
> *Now the blood*
> *Now the joyful celebration*
> *Now the wedding*
> *Now the songs*
> *Now the heart forgiven leaping*
> *Now the Spirit's visitation*
> *Now the Son's epiphany*
> *Now the Father's blessing*
> *Now*
> *Now*
> *Now*

In this one simple verse Jaroslav Vajda sums up an hour on Sunday morning. He begins with our approach to God: "Now the empty hands uplifted." We can bring nothing to God. All we have and who we are is a result of God's grace in our lives. "Now the kneeling/Now the plea" is our confession of sin, a confession that does not go for naught. "Now the Father's arms in welcome" is reminiscent of Jesus' parable of the Prodigal Son. No matter how wasteful the son was, the father welcomed him with opened arms, a joyful heart, and a fatted calf when the son eventually returned home. Even so our heavenly Father welcomes us back after the wastes in our lives.

The word proclaimed is summed up with "Now the hearing/Now the pow'r." The Gospel creates and strengthens faith. Silently, silently God works in our hearts through his Word. The power may not seem significant, but it is a power that raises the dead to life, gives new life to downtrodden people, and made 11 fearful disciples bold proclaimers of the Kingdom. This Word also creates faith and life in stone cold hearts and can create and nurture faith even in babies.

The communion with our Lord is expressed in "Now the body/Now the blood/Now the joyful celebration." Our Lord becomes one with us in a most intimate way-the body he gave and the blood he shed on Calvary becomes one with us as our sins are forgiven in a personal manner! How God does this we cannot explain, but His Word says this is so.

After this we leave in joy. Vajda uses imagery of the joy of our forgiveness and our status as children of God: wedding, songs, leaping. Have you ever seen anyone sad at a wedding? I have DJ'ed a number of weddings and I have yet to see anyone at a reception who was depressed. Rather, people dance to music they wouldn't normally even listen to. Songs are a symptom of joy, not sadness. There is a saying: "I have a song in my heart." And how many people are leaping when they are sad? Leaping for joy means you have joy.

Vajda ends his brief hymn with a benediction, starting, oddly enough, with the Holy Spirit. As the creeds state, the three persons are "co-equal and co-eternal." Vajda also tells us when these blessings are ours: "Now/Now/Now." We are not only looking for the vague, sometime in the future eternity, but we know God works in our lives even now, creating a new life as he works through Word and Sacrament.

Then the Glory

> *Then the glory*
> *Then the rest*
> *Then the Sabbath peace unbroken*
> *Then the garden*
> *Then the throne*
> *Then the crystal river flowing*
> *Then the splendor*
> *Then the life*
> *Then the new creation singing*
> *Then the marriage*
> *Then the love*
> *Then the feast of joy unending*
> *Then the knowing*
> *Then the light*
> *Then the ultimate adventure*
> *Then the Spirit's harvest gathered*
> *Then the Lamb in majesty*
> *Then the Father's Amen*
> *Then*

Then
Then

I realize I am using a hymnal edited by others. Is it possible these two hymns were meant to be part of a complete hymn? Are there other hymns/verses following this pattern extant?

This hymn looks forward to the coming Kingdom after the Judgment Day. And Vajda uses the images Jesus used in his parables on heaven.

The opening lines refer back to creation. The Sabbath peace refers to the seventh day when God rested from his creation activity. The word "Sabbath" is actually a Hebrew word meaning "rest;" it does not mean Saturday. Which day of the week we choose for our Sabbath rest is not mandated by Scripture. It is a foretaste of our eternal rest in heaven.

The garden, the throne, and the river hearken back to the Garden of Eden, when mankind ruled the earth with God and the rivers flowed peacefully through the garden. In an arid area like Palestine, a garden and a flowing river meant there was enough water for raising crops and nourishing the fruit of the earth. It represents an oasis from the desert of life.

"Then the marriage." In Hebrew society a marriage took place when a son finished building his house that would house his bride and him, and soon any children they may have. That was a prerequisite for marriage. But could the bridegroom just slap together a "tar paper shack?" No! His father had to inspect and approve that the house met his standards to shelter his potential grandchildren. Only then could the marriage take place. When Jesus finishes preparing a place for us, he will return and marry his bride, the Church. And with a wedding comes a feast-this time a feast of joy unending!

"Then the knowing/Then the light" indicates, as Paul says, "Now we see in a glass darkly." We don't know a lot about God. But we'll learn in his presence.

Vajda again ends his brief hymn with a benediction, starting again with the Holy Spirit.

Vajda also urges us patience in our Advent waiting: "Then/Then/Then."

Carol Lines to Hymn

Where Shepherds Lately Knelt

"Where Shepherds Lately Knelt,"
Christian Worship: A Lutheran Hymnal, #54

This song is another Vajda-Schalk collaboration. The basis for this hymn is the band of poor shepherds who kept watch over their flocks at night. Vajda also uses the Old Testament to describe the Messiah who fulfills the prophecies made about him.

The hymn is set the Carl Schalk tune, "Manger Song." This is a peaceful tune, no doubt it could be used as a lullaby. And isn't a lullaby an appropriate song for a baby born in a manger? Many of our Christmas hymns have that quiet, serene quality to them. They also have a quiet awe about them.

1. Where shepherds lately knelt and kept the angel's word,
    I come in half-belief, a pilgrim strangely stirred;
    But there is room and welcome there for me,
    But there is room and welcome there for me.
2. In that unlikely place I find him as they said:
    Sweet newborn Babe, how frail! And in a manger bed,
    A still small voice to cry one day for me,
    A still small voice to cry one day for me.
3. How should I not have known Isaiah would be there,
    His prophecies fulfilled? With pounding heart I stare:
    A child, a son, the Prince of Peace for me,
    A child, a son, the Prince of Peace for me.
4. Can I, will I forget how Love was born, and burned
    It's way into my heart unasked, unforced, unearned,
    To die, to live, and not alone for me,
    To die, to live, and not alone for me.

You may notice that Vajda uses repetition. In this hymn he repeats the last thought of each verse twice. (The last two hymns in this book repeated a single word: "Now" and "Then.")

Vajda goes back to that hill in Judea, that inn in Bethlehem, that stable with its now-famous manger by that inn. There is irony in this hymn. He places himself as a pilgrim coming with the shepherds, seemingly half-believing what the angel had just told them. The first verse is an ironic twist to Luke's statement: "And she laid him in a manger, because there was no room for them in the inn." Vajda tells us that for him there is room in this baby's Kingdom for him, and not only room, but he is welcome to be there. That is a nice twist on Luke's account, no?

In verse two Vajda mentions the unlikeliness of finding a royal baby where he found him—in a manger, where animals eat. And the God of the universe as a baby needing the care and protection of the parents he created? How unlikely! But that's what Vajda tells us he finds in God's Word, a "still, small voice to cry one day for me." One can imagine the reflection back to Elijah who sought God's voice. Elijah listened to a fierce wind, a raging fire, and loud thunder, but did not hear God's voice. Instead Elijah heard God's voice in a still, small voice. (1 Kings 19:9-14) And even today God speaks in a still, small voice. He speaks through his Word and his Sacraments. Simple things, really, but simple things that harness the quiet power of God.

As a note, we do well to remember God works in such small voices with great effect. We don't need to pound pulpits or fight for "righteous" legislation. We need to speak the truth in love. As Rev. Rolfe Westendorf has said many times, "If you don't speak the truth in love, you don't speak the truth." Share the hope that resides in your heart. Let God take it from there.

In verse three Vajda acknowledges Isaiah's prophecies. Isaiah is known as the Evangelist of the Old Testament. It was Isaiah who said the virgin would conceive and give birth, and that his name would be Immanuel—literally "with us is God." And stare Vajda must do, for Isaiah's prophecy lies fulfilled in that manger—a virgin, a heavenly baby, angels proclaiming peace on earth. And Vajda makes this Savior his own personal Savior.

Vajda finishes with how he is affected by that stable scene. How can anyone forget that time when Love was born? Look around you. All the world is celebrating, maybe not the true meaning of the birth, but there is definitely a conscious and concerted attempt to eradicate Christ from the celebration from the generic "Happy Holidays" and holiday trees and parades to the absence of Christ in most new Christmas songs. But Vajda says this is burned into his heart. And how does God come into our hearts? "Unasked, unforced, unearned." We were dead in trespasses, we couldn't invite Christ by nature into our hearts. But God didn't force himself in, either. He takes his time and works patiently. He sent Moses at least a dozen times to Pharoah to share the Gospel with Pharoah. God works in hearts even today, even if we cannot see that work in action. And this is unearned. This love and grace are gifts from a heavenly Father. That is why Jesus is the greatest Christmas gift ever!

Vajda ends with the purpose of that baby lying in the manger: "to die, to live, and not alone for me." Jesus is already living, so the earthly life need not be repeated. But his death and resurrection, which would form the basis of our salvation and our faith, is mentioned. But this death and resurrection isn't for a select few ("and not alone for me"). These words form a mission we take with us as we leave that place "where shepherds lately knelt."

Someone Special

"Someone Special,"
Let All the People Praise You, #54

1. Someone Special, I know who:
   That someone, my God, is you!
   Who could make a world like this,
   And a heaven full of bliss.
   Someone special I must be,
   Since You made it all for me!

2. Someone Special, that you are,
   To create the Christmas star,
   Heralding the Savior's birth,
   Bringing peace and joy to earth.
   Someone special I must be,
   Since You made that Star for me!

3. Someone Special, who would give
   His own Son that all might live,
   And by Him would set us free
   From all sin and misery.
   Someone special I must be,
   Since You gave Your Son for me!

4. Someone Special, who would send
   His good Spirit for a Friend,
   Faith Creator, Light and Guide,
   Always standing at my side.
   Someone special I must be,
   Since You gave that Gift to me!

5. Someone special-God and man,
   You were there when I began,
   You'll be there when I depart,
   For You live within my heart.
   Someone special-now I see,
   That someone is really me.

This song is another Vajda collaboration with Carl Schalk. This song explains why Christmas came about-because we are special!

The first verse explains that God himself is special. Why is God special? Because we acknowledge that he is the creator of heaven and earth. Notice how Vajda poetically describes the work of God the Father as defined in the First Article of the Creed?

The second verse reminds us of God's promise of a Savior. This promise was made right after Adam and Eve fell into sin. God didn't say, "Oops, we have a mistake. Now give me some time to come up with a solution." Nor did God say, "Well, now, you two have to figure out how to make this right again. Any solutions?" Instead, God first gave Adam and Eve an opportunity to come clean: "Where are you?" "Who told you that you were naked?" "Did you eat from that tree I told you not to eat from?" Of course Adam blamed Eve, Eve blamed the serpent, and everyone shifts the blame. Still, God didn't call the whole thing off. St. Paul eloquently puts it when he wrote to the Ephesians:

For he chose us in him before the creation of the world to be holy and blameless in his sight. In love he predestined us to be adopted as his sons through Jesus Christ, in accordance with his pleasure and will-to the praise of his glorious grace, which he has freely given us in the One he loves. In him we have redemption through his blood, the forgiveness of sins, in accordance with the riches of God's grace that he lavished on us with all wisdom and understanding. And he made known to us the mystery of his will according to his good pleasure, which he purposed in Christ, to be put into effect when the times will have reached their fulfillment-to bring all things in heaven and on earth together under one head, even Christ. (Galatians 1:4-10)

Which is what Vajda describes in verse 3, the Son sent to set us free. Jesus came as part of the "grand plan" designed before the world came into existence. I like to remind people that God knew who we would be and all the nasty things we would do before he created the world and before he created us. But he created anyway. And he loves us anyway. He loved us enough to send his Only Son—the baby we see in the manger.

In verse 4 Vajda brings in the Holy Spirit, thus finishing the Trinity. One cannot help but know that Vajda believes fervently in the Trinity. It is the Holy Spirit that brings us to faith in the Savior and strengthens that faith until God calls us home.

In verse 5 Vajda could have simply said, "Immanuel." But then he would have no rhyme or meter. So he poetically describes Immanuel and concludes that God thinks of us all as special. For proof, look at the gift given from God. God gave his One and Only Son to be sin for us. He did this so that we might not die, but live.

As a special creation of God, take joy in the gifts he gives you, lean on Him in times of trouble and sorrow, and have faith in the Greatest Gift which gives us peace.

It seems Vajda wrote some verses to this hymn honoring teachers. I add them here for your enjoyment.

- TEACHERS PAST-
  1. Someone special, teachers past,
     Teaching truths that last and last,
     Planting seeds they prayed would grow,
     Yet not reaping what they sowed,
     Someone special they must be,
     For those seeds bore fruit in me.
- TEACHERS PRESENT-
  2. Someone special, teachers now,
     Teaching God's own "why" and "how,"
     Pointing to the Word who came,
     Everlastingly the same:,
     Someone special they must be,
     In whom creed and life agree.
- TEACHERS FUTURE-
  3. Someone special still to come,
     Marching to a distant drum,
     Children now, some day mature,
     What they teach will long endure:,
     Someone special they will be,
     Everyone a fruitful tree.

Carol Lines to Hymn

Before the Marvel of This Night

"Before the Marvel of This Night,"
Let All the People Praise You, #54

1. Before the marvel of this night
   Adoring, fold your wings and bow,
   Then tear the sky apart with light
   And with your news the world endow.
   Proclaim the birth of Christ and peace,
   That fear and death and sorrow cease:
   Sing peace, sing peace, sing gift of peace.
   Sing peace, sing gift of peace.

2. Awake the sleeping world with song,
   This is the day the Lord has made.
   Assemble here, celestial throng,
   In royal splendor come arrayed.
   Give earth a glimpse of heav'nly bliss,
   A teasing taste of what they miss:
   Sing bliss, sing bliss, sing endless bliss.
   Sing bliss, sing endless bliss.

3. The love that we have always known,
   Our constant joy and endless light,
   Now to the loveless world be shown,
   Now break upon its deathly night.
   Into one song compress the love,
   That rules our universe above:
   Sing love, sing love, sing God is love.
   Sing love, sing God is love.

On Christmas Eve we join with Jaroslav Vajda in beholding the "marvel of this night." And for this marvel Vajda takes us back to "where the shepherds lately knelt" to observe the song of the angels.

You will again observe that Vajda uses repetition. Each verse ends with a phrase that is repeated. And again the composer is Carl Schalk.

The hymn begins with the angels preparing then singing their song for the shepherds. And first the angels honor Him who set in motion our redemption. They fold their wings and bow. But the news is too beautiful and too joyful to keep contained. The angels tear the sky apart with light! They get to proclaim peace. They get to proclaim that sin and death will cease, that sin and death no longer hold dominion over God's creation.

Sing gift of peace!

Alas, should the angels awaken anyone at night? Wouldn't this be considered rude? Let's rephrase this. If a family member or close friend had a baby, would you be mad or disappointed if that person called you late at night or in the wee early hours to break the news? I doubt it. You would be overjoyed! And thus the angels are encouraged and invited to come and share the Good News. For in this sight and in this message we get a glimpse of heavenly bliss.

Sing endless bliss!

In verse three Vajda shares with us that this Good News is too good to keep to ourselves. Like the shepherds we, too, want to share what we have seen and heard. We are to share this love to a loveless world. We are to break the night with celestial light. And notice, we don't have to be eloquent or learned or trained in a theological seminary. We can compress the message of love into one song-just like the angels did. That one, brief song encapsulates the essence of God's redemption: Promise fulfilled.

Vajda uses St. John's description of God: God is love. And that is what we sing in our compressed song of grace.

Sing God is love.

May this Christmas bring peace to your heart knowing the baby whose birth we celebrate came of his own volition that we might be redeemed and live with him for all eternity. He gave up his heavenly home so that he could share eternity with all of us.

Carol Lines to Hymn

John L. Hoh, Jr.

The King the Wise Men Found

"The King the Wise Men Found"

Chorus:
> The king the wise men found in Bethlehem
> Was the King they came to worship-the Messiah.
> We now make that same glad journey
> As we worship You with them.

1. From a foreign land afar we come to see You
   In our deep dark night You send a Star to guide us.
   Promised Morning Star, announce the new day's dawning;
   Glowing in our hearts, Your light will never fail us. (Chorus)

2. To the holy Child who came to earth from heaven
   We present the gift of myrrh, a sign of sadness.
   Long-awaited Star, announce the new day's dawning;
   Burning in our hearts, Your light will never fail us. (Chorus)

3. To the King of kings we worship as an infant
   We present the gift of gold fit for a monarch.
   Glory be to God and to God's most Beloved!
   Glory be on high for peace and love on earth!

In looking for an Epiphany hymn written by Vajda I came up empty. One may exist, but I couldn't find it. I did find this translation of a Puerto Rican carol, however, on *The Marvel of This Night*, the CD issued by Concordia Publishing House featuring, as it claims, "The Christmas Heart of Jaroslav Vajda." And this delightful hymn would be good to study this Epiphany.

Epiphany has traditionally been reserved to celebrate the coming of the wise men recorded by Matthew. These men are well-known as part of the Christmas story, but the details of these men are unknown to us. Matthew simply says, "Wise men from the east saw a star." Matthew goes on to record they went West to Jerusalem to seek out the new "king of the Jews." So, who were these men?

Traditionally, we think of three men ("We three kings of orient are"). We assume they are Gentiles. Often, we think of them as kings.

However, Matthew does not tell us how many men came. Three is a nice number, probably owing to the fact that three gifts were brought for Christ: gold, frankincense, and myrrh. These gifts are important as they spell out the three-fold office of God's Messiah. Gold was tribute given to a King. Frankincense was used by prophets when they offered prayers to God, thus the Wise Men acknowledged a Prophet in Bethlehem. Myrrh was a burial spice and Christ's role a Priest was to offer himself once as the sacrifice for all. All three substances were rare and costly. No doubt they came in handy when the Holy Family lived in exile in Egypt (and we do not know how long that exile was).

Can we assume the wise men were Gentiles? Traditionally they were considered Gentiles, thus the Church has handily seen Christmas Day as God's fulfillment of his Old Testament prophecies and Epiphany was seen as the manifestation of that Promise to the Gentiles. Yet, they could have been Jews. Not all Jews returned to Judea after the Babylonian/Persian Captivity. Many stayed behind in the Persian Empire. Remember also that the ten Northern tribes had the word of God and the Promise. Maybe the wise men were from this remnant. It would seem unlikely (although not impossible) for Gentiles to see a significance in a star and then head for Jerusalem. Again, Matthew doesn't tell us. A clue might be found in the book of Daniel where Daniel is identified as a "wise man," a "magi."

Were they kings? Certainly kings could have afforded such extravagant gifts. Very few commoners would have been able to afford the gifts that were brought. However, they could have gone to Jerusalem with their king(s) blessing(s) and been bestowed these gifts. Royalty honors royalty. Again, Matthew only refers to them as "Magi."

Let's assume there were three Gentile kings. It would tailor nicely into the "inclusive tent" that is Christianity.

And as a Lutheran I can move beyond the Germanic-Nordic roots of my faith to include this beautiful carol from my Hispanic brothers and sisters in the faith in Puerto Rico.

The chorus tells us about the King, the center of our worship. The Magi sought him. We seek him. Ergo, this King ties the church together as one family, one Kingdom, one faith.

The first verse speaks of coming from a foreign land. The wise men, obviously, came from afar. And Puerto Rico to Jerusalem and Bethlehem is also a fair distance (one that would require planes, trains, and automobiles). But is this a distance merely of physical space—or also of spiritual separation between God and man? That, too, is a distance that needs to be bridged. The clue comes as the verse goes on. The carol speaks of our dark night to which is sent the Morning Star.

The Morning Star. I was in college before I was aware of the identity of the morning star. I assumed it was the sun. Then I learned it was Venus. Microsoft Encarta states:

> *Except for the sun and the moon, Venus is the brightest object in the sky. The planet is called the morning star when it appears in the east at sunrise, and the evening star when it is in the west at sunset. In ancient times the evening star was called Hesperus and the morning star Phosphorus or Lucifer. Because of the distances of the orbits of Venus and earth from the sun, Venus is never visible more than three hours before sunrise or three hours after sunset. ("Venus (planet)," Microsoft (R) Encarta. Copyright (c) 1994 Microsoft Corporation. Copyright (c) 1994 Funk & Wagnall's Corporation.)*

The carol looks at the morning star aspect of Venus, that is it brings the first light of a new day. And certainly Christ's birth brings a new day for our salvation. God has kept his promise! (Messiah, Christ) His son has come to save us from our sin! (Jesus) God is now with us! (Immanuel) And this light glows in our hearts, never to fail us.

The second verse speaks of the baby's purpose—a purpose presaged by the gift of myrrh. Myrrh was used as a spice when burying a body. Thus the baby's purpose, to die for sins, is seen in such a macabre gift. To illustrate how macabre this gift was, it would be like presenting a new mother with fully-paid arrangements at a local funeral home for a baby shower gift. But God's eternal plan was to send his Son to die for our sins. Hence in this case the gift is not out of place.

Notice how the mention of the star is made, but not specifically to the visit by the Magi?

The final verse brings the aspect of royalty with the gift of gold. And the paradox is stunning—we worship a simple baby in simple circumstances as the King of all. Who would have thought? Yes, we do honor royal babies, especially the first-born of a monarch who is anticipated to take the throne. But that is all—we recognize their potential. They are no kings or queens, but merely potential rulers. But in that baby in Bethlehem we see a ruler who rules the universe even as he lays helpless in his mother's arms. Imagine the trust Jesus had to have in his Father to protect while he was very vulnerable. I don't think we stress this aspect of Jesus' obedience to God's will and his trust in his heavenly Father.

The verse ends with an echo of the song sung by the angels on that first Noel.

May your Epiphany be blessed as you realize how our Lord is manifest in your life. For Epiphany means "to make manifest" or "to reveal oneself in glory." During this season Jesus manifests himself as the eternal Son of God. He also manifests himself in our lives since he became our brother.

Carol Lines to Hymn

John L. Hoh, Jr.

Go, My Children, With my Blessing

"Go, My Children, With my Blessing,"
Let All the People Praise You, #54

1. Go, My children, with My blessing, Never alone.
   Waking, sleeping, I am with you; You are My own.
   In My love's baptismal river I have made you Mine forever.
   Go, My children, with My blessing, You are My own.

2. Go, My children, sins forgiven, At peace and pure.
   Here you learned how much I love you, What I can cure.
   Here you heard My dear Son's story; Here you touched Him,
   saw His glory.
   Go, My children, sins forgiven, At peace and pure.

3. Go, My children, fed and nourished, Closer to Me;
   Grow in love and love by serving, Joyful and free.
   Here My Spirit's power filled you; Here His tender comfort
   stilled you.
   Go, My children, fed and nourished, Joyful and free.

4. I the Lord will bless and keep you And give you peace;
   I the Lord will smile upon you And give you peace;
   I the Lord will be your Father, Savior, Comforter, and
   Brother.
   Go, My Children; I will keep you And give you peace.

A beautiful hymn for New Year's Eve is this one Jaroslav
Vajda wrote as a benediction. In a departure from many of
his other hymns, this one is not set to a Carl Schalk
composition. It uses a Welsh lullaby, a tune I have heard
on CDs of lullabies we bought when my son was born. (I
have included the lyrics to one, called "All Through the
End," at the end of this chapter.)

In verse one Vajda relates to us the claim God can make
about us and the care he has for us. God is with us
"waking and sleeping." And God has made us his through
the baptismal water. Luther often said that he never said
that he was baptized but that he is baptized. In Luther's
mind, that seemingly one-time action has life-long
consequences. God keeps the promises made through that
baptism, promises to remain with us, to create and
strengthen faith through that baptism. In summary, that
though we might change after our baptism, God remains
changeless and remains faithful to his promises and to us.

Verse two is a benediction of what we learn and take from
God's Word. The setting in this hymn is the church service
where we learn about God's amazing grace. It can also refer
to those informal moments when we study God's Word—
personal study, small group Bible classes, family devotions,
in our prayer life, among other times.

In verse three the Trinity is identified by their actions we
know them by: Father in our preservation (including the
food for the Spirit); the Son who personifies love, from

which and for whom we serve; and the Spirit who fills us with his power and gives us comfort, again from God's Word.

Does verse four sound familiar? Try this:

> *The Lord bless you and keep you;*
> *The Lord make his face shine upon you and be gracious to you;*
> *The Lord turn his face toward you and give you peace.*
> *(Numbers 6:24-26)*

Yes, it's the Aaronic blessing. You may have heard it every Sunday at the close of each church service. This was the blessing God wished his priests to speak to the Children of Israel. God wants his people to know he loves them and seeks to bless them and shine upon them.

Ever wonder about that term "make his face shine upon you?" When someone is very happy and excited about something, that person's face shines. Once, when I was laid off, I had out-placement counseling. One of the workouts was to have a brief interview with a coach and discuss our previous job and our family. The coach mentioned at the end of the exercise that he saw my face light up when I began talking about my son. Wow! God has the same love and joy for and about me that I have for my son! Doesn't that give you comfort?

I felt this hymn was appropriate for New Years. We again face another year as we always do, both with joy and uncertainty. May your New Year be blessed in the knowledge and comfort of sins forgiven, that you are a child of God.

"All Through the Night"

This Welsh lullaby has religious overtones and could be added to the Vajda piece. It speaks of a benediction and prayer for a child about to fall asleep. It speaks of angel protection for the child. Notice the repetition, common with folk songs and lullabies.

1. Sleep my child and peace attend thee,
   All through the night
   Guardian angels God will send thee,
   All through the night
   Soft the drowsy hours are creeping
   Hill and vale in slumber sleeping,
   I my loving vigil keeping
   All through the night.

2. While the moon her watch is keeping
   All through the night
   While the weary world is sleeping
   All through the night
   O'er thy spirit gently stealing
   Visions of delight revealing
   Breathes a pure and holy feeling
   All through the night.

3. Love, to thee my thoughts are turning
   All through the night
   All for thee my heart is yearning,
   All through the night.
   Though sad fate our lives may sever
   Parting will not last forever,
   There's a hope that leaves me never,
   All through the night.

Christmas Carol Answers

1. The initial example of a highly celebrated nativity: **The First Noel**

2. A felicitous emotion, directed at the entirety of the terrestrial sphere: **Joy to the World**

3. Pass hitherward, everyone who exhibits consistency of character: **O Come, all ye Faithful**

4. A young lad whose musical talents are expressed rhythmically: **Little Drummer Boy**

5. The hour of its transparent occurrence coincided with the instant often associated with maximal darkness, either figurative or literal: **It Came Upon a Midnight Clear**

6. Strike with the fist, with sufficient force as to cause unconsciousness, Mr. and Mrs. Hall: **Deck the Halls**

7. A nocturnal period unbroken by auditory interruptions: **Silent Night**

8. My advice to you is to listen intently to, and heed, the heavenly messengers as they vocalize musical selections announcing an important event: **Hark! The Herald Angels Sing**

9. A significant distance from here, within the confines of a feeding trough for animals: **Away in a Manger**

10. The auditory sensation of roughly spherical sound-making objects, vibrating in a resonant fashion, followed by the name of the objects themselves: **Jingle Bells**

11. Our sincere desire for you is for your yuletide celebration to be an enjoyable one: **We Wish You a Merry Christmas**

12. A dozen terrestrial rotational time periods, signifying a series of steps leading up to, and ushering in, the celebration of the Nativity: **The Twelve Days of Christmas**

13. The benevolent senior nobility whose name I shan't say because it would give away the answer to this puzzle: **Good King Wenceslaus**

14. A verbal utterance, addressed toward a coniferous member of the plant family, often used as the centerpiece of yuletide gatherings: **O, Christmas Tree**

15. Multiple highly polished, colorless, metallic, cup-shaped devices that give forth a ringing sound when struck: **Silver Bells**

16. Celestial heralds at a great altitude; specifically, those whose announcements have already been listened to and understood by us: **Angels We Have Heard on High**

17. Haste hence, and publish the news in the Alpine, Nordic, Appalachian, Rocky, and/or Himalayan regions: **Go, Tell it on the Mountain**

18. May the Almighty grant to you a recuperative repose, all you festive males of chivalrous character: **God Rest You Merry Gentlemen**

19. The original utterance, as well as a repetition, of a plea for the arrival of the One whose presence brings God Himself to us: **O Come, O Come, Emmanuel**

20. There exists in the atmosphere a musical selection: **There's a Song in the Air**

21. During the dimly-lit extent of time wherein those persons who enjoyed a bucolic relationship with the domesticated stock in their charge, monitored them for their safekeeping: **While Shepherds Watched Their Flock by Night**

22. Enlighten me as to the identity of this offspring: **What Child is This?**

23. The trio of us, the most authoritative examples of monarchical governmental leadership: **We Three Kings**

24. A temporal duration characterized by reverence, awe, and the sun's position being beneath the horizon: **O Holy Night**

25. From a celestial locale, one over our heads, to a terrestrial locale I arrive: **From Heav'n Above to Earth I Come**

www.ingramcontent.com/pod-product-compliance
Lightning Source LLC
Chambersburg PA
CBHW030419100426

42812CB00028B/3025/J